T0197807

I  Me

featuring the "my bad" bunch!

By

Andrea Bierria

MS.Sped & Ms.Ed, life coach & yoga instructor. Aspiring Actress.

AuthorHouse™
1663 Liberty Drive
Bloomington, IN 47403
www.authorhouse.com
Phone: 833-262-8899

This book is printed on acid-free paper.

ISBN: 978-1-6655-1776-8 (sc)
ISBN: 978-1-6655-1777-5 (e)

Library of Congress Control Number: 2021903712

Print information available on the last page.

Published by AuthorHouse 03/31/2021

authorHOUSE®

I ♥ Me

featuring the "my bad" bunch!

Table of Contents

FOREWORD

The purpose of this book is to help build your confidence. To help build a clear purpose for your life. This book is dedicated to all future middle schoolers who are seeking guidance on how to tackle this big gigantic confusing world. First and foremost, always seek advice from a responsible adult such as it be your parents, grandparents, or other guardians in your life a god parent or a favorite aunt or uncle, or even your favorite teacher. And never keep secrets from your parents or guardians keeping secrets means you have something to hide and your too young to hide things. There is no situation that you have encountered, that you cannot share with someone. If you are approached by anyone even someone you know, to keep a secret, talk, talk and talk to someone.

Our first activity is for you to pick out a name for yourself that explains one of your best attributes. My name is Andrea, so I choose to call myself amazing Andrea. The word amazing begins with the letter A and so does my name. The word amazing is how I feel about myself. My talents, my smile, my laugh, and my personality. Can you think of an acronym that begins with the first letter of your name? Let's say your name begins with A and you chose Amazing Abby, why are you amazing, I am amazing because I like to help people. I like to walk my dog, or I like to watch tv with my grandparents, whatever you feel makes you special. Remember, I love me means just that. I love me! For whatever reason you choose. Doing a good deed does make us feel special and helpful, but sometimes it's small things that makes a big deal. Like telling someone how much they mean to you, and saying the word thank you and please really gives you a badge of honor. Those words make you a hero! If you were in my yoga class, I would consider you a warrior! A warrior is a real nice person who is confident and stands firm in their beliefs. Now, Let us see your warrior stance!

Our next activity is to write a mission statement that creates goals and boundaries. I believe that I am great, I can do all things. That I am allowed to do left! I respect myself; I respect others, I respect who I am and who I strive to be.

My vision statement allows you to see yourself, even at your age you can see yourself as the best volleyball player or jump rope jumper.

My vision statement is I see myself climbing mountains. Breaking down barriers. Rising to the top my game. I see myself happy and living my best life! As you write your vision statement, think of something that you like to do. If you like playing basketball, dancing, rapping, or cooking, babysitting. Write down what you like to do and why? Practice makes perfect, so whatever your hobby is, perfect it means practice as much as you can to get better. Remember boys and girl's schoolwork comes first!

Now you should be able to write your mission statement and your vision statement in your journal. And remember to use your special name you picked for yourself, example, I Am amazing Andrea my mission is to….and I am amazing Andrea, I vision myself….

MISSION STATEMENT

Name:

Mission Statement:

Vision Statement:

What do I like about myself?

What makes me special?

What is my special hobby and why?

VISION BOARD

A Vision Board reminds us of our goals yes students your vision board is what you create to document what you are reaching towards. You are not expected to write your plans as a future doctor. Your goals are in your immediate future. Example: your vision board may include an obstacle you are facing that you would like to fix such as acing a math test, learning a different language etc. remember those are your goals and your goals only, you can however, talk with your parents about your vison board so they can help you achieve those goals and also monitor your progress.

Warriors make your goals attainable. This is a fun project, so warriors, have fun, and discuss something like learning to ride a bike or learning to swim with your parents, they must schedule this goal and make allowances. Remember your goals will be revisited to see how your coming along with this goal.

My vision board

My goals   **time frame**   **completion date**

I LOVE ME GLOSSARY

I love me glossary, please pick three words that pertain to you. Write a sentence that begins

with, I have or I am, you can pick your own words as well! Say these sentences each day!

**Confident**

**Self esteem**

**Courageous**

**Creative**

**Assertiveness**

**Important**

LET's MEDITATE

Okay Warriors lets meditate:

Having a bad day how about meditating, what are the benefits of meditation? To focus, have clarity, reduce anxiety, and to regulate your emotions.

Relax close your eyes (ask parents for permission)

Think of a flower that has pretty colors

As you look at the flower picture the flower growing

Or picture yourself smelling the flower

This is only done for about one- two- minutes

Birthday cake

Picture yourself at a birthday party your surrounded by your family and friends and picture a birthday cake with candles, warriors take a deep breath and blow out the candles and your done! Feel better? Well you have just set the reset button!

Warriors, what is your daily routine? Example, when I wake, I stretch my arms high towards the sky and I'm grateful for seeing another day! I brush my teeth and say hello to my family! And we eat breakfast. Halt warriors make your bed, if you have time and aren't not running late!

Sometimes warriors, if your days starts out strange or confusing, it's just for the moment it doesn't determine how your day will be. That is why it's important to get rest at night so you can have a positive morning. Why are we doing this? To start our day positively, organized and to build a routine. Thanking someone shows humility, stretching creates positive energy, and making your bed begins a routine of doing chores, which most of us do not allow our children do! Another thing you may do before you leave the house is to blow out the candles and smell the flowers. This will help us reduce stress, enhance awareness and focus your mind.

QUALITIES OF A LEADER

What are qualities of a leader? Who is your favorite leader and why?

I like Martin Luther King, he is a peace warrior, he instilled peace in the world. He dedicated his life for "everyone" to have world peace. It is important to have a leader that you admire and a person of many quotes. Example: Maya Angelou is a person of many quotes and attributes, one of her famous quotes is: I know why the caged bird sings! Or Nothing will work unless you do!

If you were a leader what type of rules would you create?

How would you convey messages of leadership skills?

Can you make up your own quote? Warriors I invite you to have fun with this portion, of "I love me"

Be silly, make up rhymes, go for it! Your quote belongs to you! So be different, be original. Why am I different?

Warriors it's ok to be different, let's say you come from another country, or from another school. Everyone wants to be liked and feel welcomed sometimes when you're the new kid on the block you might feel that you're not accepted by your peers, colleagues, neighbors, we can celebrate diversity by welcoming our new friends, bullying and teasing is played out, no one's doing that anymore. Most of us have diversified backgrounds, my father's side of the family comes from Cuba, New Orleans and my mothers' side of my family is Puerto Rican.

School integration-invite the students to talk about where he or she comes from!

School curriculum-draw a flag, talk about national dishes.

Community connection- invite newcomers to community meeting and outings and let's celebrate diversity together!

WHY AM I ALWAYS SO ANGRY?

Warriors, sometimes there are things going on beyond our control! It's not your Fault!

Shake it off! Do not carry your situations/problems to school or take out your anger

against anyone and if you do please apologize immediately! Do not let your problems

deter you from becoming great! There are plenty of resources to help you deal and cope

with your situation. What can you do to help diffuse your anger?

Suggestions:

Take a few minutes and just breathe in and out .

Possibly walk away from the anger point.

Talk with someone.

Hit the Reset button, do not hold on to anger.

FINAL MESSAGE

Okay Warriors here is the final message in the I love me series 1st handbook! This may be a little graphic, but this is a true story, sometimes hopefully not, you might come across some of the cooler kids who may seem that they got it going on! As we said in my day! And in the mist of having fun and being a tween or teen, you might find yourself having to make a choice, only you can make that choice, but will it be the right choice?

Jenn: Hi Lynn

Tobias: Hey you two, want to cut class?

Jen: Well cutting is bad

Tobias: Ah come on, well be back in time for the bus!

Jenn: I can't I got into so much trouble, the last time, my mom was furious, and I had double chores and no phone, no thank you!

Lynn: I am down!

Tobias: Great! Let's go!

Jen: Bye (Jenn walks to class)

Lynn: Ok where we headed?

Tobias: We are going to meet up with Ely

Lynn: But Ely well ah, likes to steal.

Tobias: He never got caught, and it's not proven

Lynn: Well everyone thinks he is a thief and that is bad!

Tobias: Who cares what everybody thinks.

Lynn: Well what are we doing?

Tobias: We just chilling playing the games and whatever!

They meet up with Ely

Ely: Hey what's up welcome to the cut class house dweebs. Lol

Lynn: Hey what's up!

Tobias: You got food dude

Ely: No, this is not the cafeteria

Lynn: Thank Goodness!

Tobias: Well I am hungry let's walk to the store.

Lynn: Who has money

Ely: Not I said the poor guy

Tobias: Not I but I have an idea.

Tthey get to the store and huddle and talk about their plan.

Lynn walks in and distracts the manager /store clerk and ask about an item.

Ely and Tobias go in the store after Lynn and are circling around in different directions.

Lynn is still trying to distract the clerks.

However, the clerk gets suspicious and starts looking at the two boys,

Although they had nothing in their hands or pockets, they all start screaming go!

The three make a dash for the door. As soon as they come outside, the police were in front of the store.

They had not taken anything from the store, but why go to the store if you have no money?

They get questioned and their parents were called of course they were cutting class. The

store bans them from coming in without their parents, and until after school hours. Their

parents were disappointed, and the trio had to promise they would not do it again. Oh,

and the parents informed the store clerk that since their kids like going to the store so

much how about letting them throw out the garbage and sweep the place for a week!

<u>Reflection:</u>

What choices can you make? Are the crowd of friends you have make good choices? Or tend to like to break rules, encourage them to make good choices and walk away from trouble. If someone says let's cut school—

Think of your actions and what the consequences would be!

The moral of the story is please watch the crowd your with. Lynn knew her friends were

trouble and she went anyway.

The End!

DEDICATION PAGE

I dedicate this book to all the warriors of the Universe!

Stand Tall Warriors!

I dedicate this book to my children Brandon, Justin, my nephews Andre, Arin, Bryson and Nieces, Racine and Faythe. And my mom Helen, Ms. Lester and Ms. Minatee and all my besties! Barrios and Sanchez, Mrs. Walker, Mrs. Grant, Esperanza, The Bierria's, The Smith's , The Walker Family, Marcelin, Tollazo's, Reyes Family and Sanchez Family

My sis Denise, April, Diane, Beanie, Niecey, Sue, Monique, Syeda, Jill, Caraissia, Badria, Melody, Val, Bro Sha, Cesare, Quentin, Jimmy, Lusaka, Angie, Tori, Sandra, Zenobia, Taleta, Olga, Taisha, Jeannie, Stephanie, Gem, Precious, Felicia, Duck, Tawana, Camille, TeeTee, Dyan, Kenya, Elaine, Ronis, Renee, Natasha, Yvonne, Bird, Omari, Mr. Gold, Marvisa, Almay and Michelle

To my step daughters Ajahnae, Santina Shelana and Gabriella

The love of my life my husband Charles Watson. And my stepdaughter, Gabriella Watson a future warrior! and the entire Watson Family, I love you all!

I also want to thank My prayer line Family, My Yoga Family! Sis Connie and Minister Desiree, You two are awesome! Rinnay, Carrie, Vanessa, Stephanie, Sammoria, Almethia, Denise, Pastor Powell, Brother Curtis and Mellisa, Karen and Cheryl

All my places of work, Internships and Trainings, to David and Nan! My acting Coaches-Will Gilly Productions

Newburgh Enlarged School District

Breathe for Change, Board of Education. YMCA

Boys and Girls Club

Girl Scouts of America

Boys Scouts of America

Charlie William Chris & the fire man

Brandon and Justin

Brother Curtis! Hit that reset button. Thank You.

Young & Unique Christian Daycare

Restore Your Power Tutoring Service

Walden Police Department

Law Offices of Sobo & Sobo

Ouimette Goldstein & Andrews LLP

Jerry's Kitchen

Kim's Soul food Restaurant

G and H Deli

Eddys Jerk Center

Fish & Chikzz

One Stop Manufacturing service

Dr. Dassa Orthopedic Medical Service

Rommel Millian Physical Therapy

My Churches:

Andre Cook Ministries

Greater Love Deliverance Church

Walden Baptist Church

Mount Carmel Church of Christ

Tabernacle of Faith Christian Fellowship

Best Temple Church of God in Christ

Ebenezer Baptist Church

New Life Pentecostal Church

And Thank You. AuthorHouse.

Dedicated to all those who lost their lives due to CoVid-19

In Memory of Crystal, J.C, Dotty, Miguel, Sam, Mildred, Ebony, Mrs. Virginia, Stephanie, Karen, Grandma Isabel, Grandma Rose, Carlos Sanchez, Steve, Ms. Depass, Norma, and Johnny.

Printed in the United States
by Baker & Taylor Publisher Services